Contents

Words shown in the text in bold, **like this**, are explained in the Glossary.

Who was Martin Luther King Jr.?

Martin Luther King Jr. was a black American **preacher**. He spent his life trying to make life better for black American people.

Martin Luther King Jr. was a brave man. He was one of the greatest Americans in history.

The Life of
Martin Luther King Jr.

Emma Lynch

Heinemann
LIBRARY

www.heinemann.co.uk/library

Visit our website to find out more information about **Heinemann Library** books.

To order:
 Phone 44 (0) 1865 888066
 Send a fax to 44 (0) 1865 314091
Visit the Heinemann Bookshop at www.heinemann.co.uk/library to browse our catalogue and order online.

First published in Great Britain by Heinemann Library, Halley Court, Jordan Hill, Oxford OX2 8EJ, part of Harcourt Education.
Heinemann is a registered trademark of Harcourt Education Ltd.

Editorial: Lucy Thunder and Harriet Milles
Design: Richard Parker and
       Tinstar Design Ltd (www.tinstar.co.uk)
Illustration: Gerry Ball
Picture Research: Melissa Allison and Fiona Orbell
Production: Camilla Smith

Originated by Repro Multi-Warna
Printed and bound in China by
    South China Printing Company
The paper used to print this book comes from sustainable resources.

ISBN 0 431 18095 4
09 08 07 06 05
10 9 8 7 6 5 4 3 2 1

ISBN 0 431 18155 1
10 09 08 07 06
10 9 8 7 6 5 4 3 2 1

British Library Cataloguing in Publication Data
Emma Lynch
Martin Luther King Jr. – (The Life of)
323.1'196073 ' 092
A full catalogue record for this book is available from the British Library.

Acknowledgements
The Publishers would like to thank the following for permission to reproduce photographs:
p. **4** Getty Images/Hulton Archive; p. **6** James Randklev/Corbis; pp. 7, 8 Sean Victory/Harcourt Education Ltd.; p. **9** Corbis; p. **10** Getty Images; pp. **11**, **12**, **15**, **16**, **18**, **24** Corbis/Bettman; pp. **13**, **20**, **23** Flip Schulke/Corbis; pp. **14**, **21**, **22**, **27** AP Wide World Photos; p. **17** Getty Images/Time Life Pictures; p. **25** Popperfoto; p. **26** Richard Cummins/Corbis

Cover photograph of Martin Luther King Jr., reproduced with permission of Getty Images/Time Life Pictures. Page icons: Hemera PhotoObjects.

The Publishers would like to thank Rebecca Vickers for her assistance in the preparation of this book.

Martin worked peacefully. He did not use **violence** to get what he wanted. He led **protest marches** and **boycotts** to fight for a better life for black people.

This map shows some of places where Martin lived and worked in the USA.

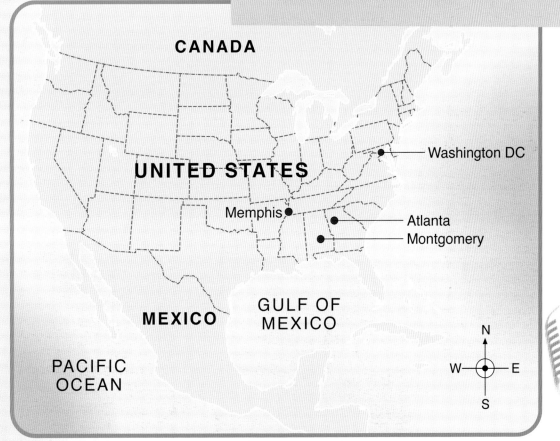

CANADA

UNITED STATES

Washington DC

Memphis

Atlanta

Montgomery

MEXICO

GULF OF MEXICO

PACIFIC OCEAN

N
W E
S

Martin's childhood

Martin Luther King Jr. was born on 15 January 1929, in Atlanta, Georgia, USA. His father was a **minister** and his mother had been a school teacher.

Martin Luther King Jr. was born in this house.

Martin played with black friends and white friends who lived near by.

Martin had many hobbies when he was a boy. He liked to play **baseball** and football. He also liked to ride his bicycle and play with kites and model planes.

Separate schools

There were no white children at Martin's school. The **law** in the southern states of USA said that children with different skin colours could not go to the same school.

There were only black children at Martin's school.

Martin was a very clever boy. His school marks were always good. He was able to go to Morehouse College in Atlanta, Georgia when he was only 15 years old.

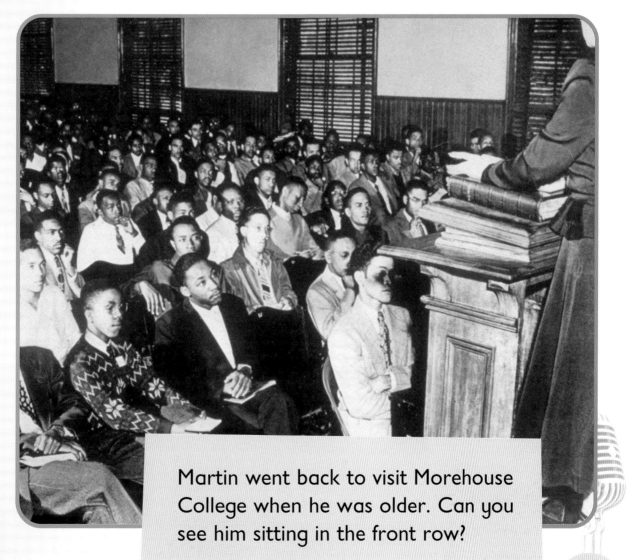

Martin went back to visit Morehouse College when he was older. Can you see him sitting in the front row?

Working for the Church

Martin wanted to be a church **minister** when he grew up. When he was 17 years old, he gave a **sermon** in his father's church.

This is Ebenezer Baptist Church in Atlanta, Georgia. Martin gave his first sermon here.

Martin learned about the work of Mohandas Gandhi. He was a famous leader in India who worked for change in peaceful ways.

Martin went to study at Crozer **Seminary** in Pennsylvania. He decided that he wanted to change the **laws** and beliefs that were unfair to black people.

Martin and Coretta

Martin then went on to study at Boston University. He met a woman in Boston called Coretta Scott. She was a singer.

Martin and Coretta were married 1953.

Martin and Coretta had four children.
Coretta gave up her singing job. She helped
Martin with his work for the rest of his life.

Coretta still liked to
sing with her children!

Trouble on the buses

In 1955, the police **arrested** a black American woman called Rosa Parks in Montgomery, Alabama. She would not give up her bus seat to a white man.

Rosa had broken the **law** in Montgomery. A policeman took her fingerprints.

Martin helped to **organize** a **boycott** of the buses. Black Americans stopped using the buses. The bus companies lost money. In 1956, the Montgomery law was dropped.

Now black people could sit where they liked on the buses. Can you see Martin in the second row?

Friends and enemies

Some white people did not like the things Martin was doing. They **bombed** Martin's house to try to stop him. In 1958, a woman tried to kill him.

Martin was badly hurt, but he got better.

Martin was now famous. He gave many speeches. He visited other countries, too. In 1959, he went to India. He wanted to talk to people who had followed Gandhi.

Martin's photo was on the cover of *Time*, an important news magazine.

Going to prison

Other black American people joined Martin in his work for people in the South. They were prepared to break unfair **laws**.

Martin was sent to prison many times.

Martin did not stop working when he was in prison. He wrote letters to people to try to change the laws. Later he wrote a book called *Stride Toward Freedom*.

Martin's book was about the bus **boycott** in Montgomery.

I have a dream ...

Martin **organized** many peaceful **protest marches.** He also gave speeches and raised a lot of money. Wherever he went, people asked him for his **autograph.**

Many people went on the protest marches.

In 1963, Martin gave a famous speech. He said, "I have a dream that one day ... little black boys and black girls will be able to join hands with little white boys and white girls as sisters and brothers."

Martin gave his famous speech in Washington DC.

A violent death

In 1964, the **Civil Rights Act** was passed. It ended some of the unfair **laws** and rules for black Americans. Martin was given a special prize for his work.

Martin received the **Nobel Peace Prize** in 1964.

On 4 April 1968, Martin was shot and killed by someone who did not like what he was doing. Martin was only 39 years old. People everywhere were shocked by his death.

Martin's son put flowers on his grave.

Why is Martin famous?

We remember Martin for his fight against unfair **laws** and beliefs. He helped to change some laws, and make life better for black American people.

Martin showed that it was possible to change people's beliefs by protesting peacefully.

Martin Luther King Jr. was a popular and brave man. He was also a great speaker. He gave black people hope and belief in a better future.

Martin's life and work is remembered because it is so important to American history.

More about Martin

We can find out more about Martin Luther King Jr. by visiting the King Center. Here we can see letters, newspapers and films about Martin's life.

The King Center is in Atlanta, Georgia.

There are many websites about Martin's life. You can find books about him in the library. Many people visit his grave in Atlanta, Georgia.

There are **memorial** statues to Martin all over the world. This one is in Westminster Abbey in London.

Fact file

- On 5 June 1955, Boston University gave Martin a special award called a 'doctorate'. This meant that Martin became called 'Doctor Martin Luther King Jr.'

- Every year, Martin Luther King Jr. Day is celebrated on the third Monday in January. This day is close to his birthday, which was on 15 January.

- James Earl Ray was sent to prison for 99 years for killing Martin.

- Nearly every major city in the United States of America has a street or a school named after Martin Luther King Jr.

Timeline

1929   Martin Luther King Jr. is born in Atlanta, Georgia on 15 January

1948   Martin becomes a **minister**

1953   Martin marries Coretta Scott

1955   The Montgomery bus **boycott** begins

1956   Martin is sent to prison for the first time

        The Montgomery bus boycott ends

1958   Martin writes Stride Toward Freedom.

        He goes to hospital after a knife attack.

1963   Martin gives his "I have a dream" speech in Washington DC

1964   The **Civil Rights Act** is passed.

        Martin is given the **Nobel Peace Prize**.

1968   Martin Luther King is killed in Memphis, Tennessee on 4 April

Glossary

arrested when the police take someone away to a police station

autograph when a famous person writes their name down for someone else

baseball game played by two teams, using a bat and a ball

bomb something that blows up

boycott to protest by refusing to do or use something

Civil Rights Act law passed to make sure all people were treated fairly

law the rules of a country

memorial something to remind us of people who have died

minister someone in charge of the people who go to church

Nobel Peace Prize awarded to people who have worked hard for change in peaceful ways

organize plan to make something happen

preacher someone who talks to people, often in church

protest marches when people walk together to complain about something that they believe is unfair

seminary college where priests train

sermon speech given in church to tell people about right and wrong

violent/violence hurting people in an angry way

Find out more

Books

I Have a Dream, Neil Tonge and Alison Astill (Hodder Children's Books, 2000)

Martin Luther King Jr. Day (True Books: Holidays), Dana Meachen Rau (Children's Press, 2001)

Meet Martin Luther King Jr. (Landmark Books), James Tertius de Kay, Jim Thomas (Ed.), (Random House Children's Books, 2001)

Websites

thekingcenter.com
Website for the King Center, set up by Coretta King, with books, photos and exhibitions about Martin and his life.

www.jeannepasero.com/mlk2.html
Martin Luther King Jr. in the classroom: contains activities, books, photographs, and posters.

Places to visit

The King Center, 449 Auburn Avenue NE, Atlanta, Georgia 30312. Tel: 001 (404) 526 8900

Index